YOU INVITED US IN

How spirits Entered My Marriage

SHANTEL D. HARRIS

ROYSTON
Publishing

**Warning: This book contains sexual
content and may trigger victims of
molestation and incest.**

BK Royston Publishing
Jeffersonville, IN 47131
http://www.bkroystonpublishing.com
bkroystonpublishing@gmail.com

Cover Design: Rachel Harper-Moore
Email: Queenthangz7@gmail.com
Facebook: Queenthang

ISBN-13: 978-1-963136-53-1

Printed in the United States of America

Dedication

This book is dedicated to my mother, the Late Evangelist Frances Thomas. Mother, you were a woman of integrity who taught me the importance of independence and strength. In the midst of teaching me independence and strength, you taught balance. Not so much independence that you feel you don't need anyone, and you are an island unto yourself. Not so much strength that pride seeps in and makes you feel it's bad to reach out for help. You were truly what the church world calls a mother in Zion. You selflessly raised your daughters as a single mother while caring for and taking into your home nieces, nephews, god kids, neighborhood kids, friends and anyone else who needed help. It makes me smile knowing that the traits I have of loving and caring for God's people come from you. You truly were a servant at heart.

Mother, although some parts of this book may be difficult to write, I move forward knowing you would be so proud. More importantly, if it helps just one person to be freed from the spirits of fear, hurt, and pain, you would be all for it.

Knowing you left your earthly vessel to enter into a place of rest and peace comforts us. Remembering your walk with God reminds me daily of why I must finish this race. You truly were a Psalm 31 woman. Alright, mama (as I called you) here we go!

In Remembrance of
The Late Evangelist Frances Thomas

"You are too beautiful and talented to waste it or let someone take advantage of it. Now, go Preach the Gospel."

My Mom's last Words to me.

ACKNOWLEDGEMENTS

It is a must that I give honor to my Lord and Savior Jesus Christ. Without Him there would be no me. Without my test and trials there would not be a testimony to help others heal. To my husband Robert Harris, you sir are truly my rock. My entire life changed when God saw fit to bring us back together after fourteen years. Without your chest to lie on and your arms to cry in there is no way I would have been able to relive my story. Thank you for allowing me to be the softest version of me. To my son, Denarius. Son your existence changed the entire trajectory of my life. I was headed down the wrong path until the day I saw you on that monitor. You were a little peanut. That day changed my life. I truly love you more than myself. Continue to be great on Purpose. To the children that God blessed me with, Angel, Wa'teria and Jael and Robert IV I am so blessed that God chose me to be your mother. In your case

Jael TT's big girl. To my best friend Apostle C.L. Roberts thank you for stepping up at the time my son and I needed you the most. We are forever grateful. Shallamar, Auntie Tina, Jasmine, Jakenya, Kristina, thank you for being my sisters. To my spiritual mother, Brenda Worlds, thank you for being a true prayer warrior. To my Entire Gracefully Broken Ministries International family, thank you for trusting me to be your Pastor. It's UP from here!

TABLE OF CONTENTS

CHAPTER 1

Grandma's House

Born in Miami, Florida, and raised in Pompano Beach, Florida, I can still smell the staleness of my grandmother's home. Anna P. Thomas. A woman of integrity, strength, and more endurance than I have ever seen. My grandmother's home was located in Collier City.

If you ever heard the locals say the name you would have no idea it was spelled that way. Ask me to spell it when I was a child, and I would have said C-A-Y-A C-I-T-Y. I think I was almost a teen when I realized how to say it correctly.

I sometimes surprised my older family members, especially my mother with how far back as a child I could remember, but I remember it like yesterday. My grandmother was actually a first-generation homeowner. She purchased her then two-bedroom, one-bathroom home, which she owned as far back as I could remember. It was definitely before my birth in 1977. That house could not have been any more than 900 square feet. If I told you how many of us lived in that house, I don't think you would believe it. My grandmother was a mother of nine. Only three to four of her children at any given time would be out of the house. The majority of the time, it was at least six of her kids along with their children living there. My mother had times when she would move us into our own home but the struggles of being a single mother with three kids would always (back then) send us back to my grandmother's house. I don't care where or how we had to sleep, grandma would not turn one child or grandchild away. Wow, back then, even her mother, my great grandmother, Lula Mae Carswell, who suffered from ailments, was in her home as well. My great grandmother is truly responsible for laying a solid foundation for my Christian walk. At the age of seven, she introduced me to the Bible by making me sit on her couch next to her and read scriptures to her.

We lived in that small home as one big happy family. My grandmother was the best cook on this side of heaven. I think we all feel that way about our grandma's food. Only it's true about mine. Ms. Pearl as everyone in the neighborhood called her, really was the best cook. I can still smell her collard greens, pan-fried cornbread made from scratch, and homemade pancakes. And her fried fish that one of the men in our family would catch or that my aunt would bring over from the Okeechobee was simply wonderful. Don't even mention how good her peach cobbler was. She only made that on special occasions. I still don't understand how the lady made all that food stretch amongst so many of us, but she did, and we were always full. The day we received food stamps was the best day ever back then. There was no card to take to the store like today. No, we had the little coupons that looked like white paper money. I can't remember which bill the purple one was, but all I know is when I got the purple one, I was able to buy lots of cookies and candy from the neighborhood storehouse. Grandma would make a list and send us to the store to get all the things she needed. We would fight over which two would go because it was guaranteed she was going to give you a brown food stamp (which was a dollar) for going. The first of the month were happy times. That meant lots of food in the house and junk like cookies and candy for us to get from the store.

Food stamp time wasn't the only time we could get candy and other junk food, though. You could also go to the store back then after collecting enough soda bottles. Man, those bottles spent like money. We would have hard-down fights over who took whose soda bottles. One soda bottle was worth ten cents. That went a long way when candy was only a penny.

We may not have been rich or even middle class. In fact, we were poor when it came to material things but definitely not when it came to family and values. And then it happened. CRACK hit our small town. It didn't just hit our town, but it took our loving little home by storm.

I would say I was around five years old when I noticed the changes in some of my aunts and uncles. When you are that young, all you know is there is a change, and it's not good. You don't know or understand why they went from being one way to being and looking totally different from what they once were. On any given day, you would see different people in and out of the little back room my grandma had recently built on the house to make more room for us. I remember seeing people walking in and out at all times of the night. White people, black people, men and women. Now that I think of it, I had never seen white people in my neighborhood unless they were police officers until the crack epidemic hit. I had only seen white folks at school or places of business. But Mr. Crack was not prejudiced. The epidemic hit homes of all colors and races. Many were affected. But back to my home. At first, it was very subtle. We would see the adults drink Bulls or Mickey's (their beer of choice), but they would never allow the kids to see them use drugs. That back room at grandma's house had so much traffic, but as a child, you just thought grandma's house was "the spot." Everyone came there to visit. It was not until the police started showing up for different incidents that you realized this was a problem.

CHAPTER 2

KIDS CAN BE CRUEL

I will never forget my first day of kindergarten. I started when I was six. Yes, I know by some of the things I have remembered thus far, you thought I was older. No. I told you in the beginning I remembered most things from a very young age. My first week of kindergarten was normal, It would take me a minute to realize it was only normal because my biological father had stopped by to give my mom money to buy new clothes and school supplies. Yes, that is what he did drop by for holidays and special occasions because he was a married man (I only knew that once I was older). My mom had three girls. None of us had the same father, and all our fathers were married. For some reason, no one in our family recognized this as wrong. We actually grew up thinking it was okay and normal. Anyhow, back to me starting school. So, the first week was normal because we were all new to the school atmosphere. It was not until about week three that the other kids began to point fingers. They realized that I was wearing the same clothes over and over, and they were dirty and unwashed. To me, this was normal. Most of the time, we played outside in the dirt and our clothes were always dirty. What was strange to them was my norm. Every now and then, my mom would send us to the laundromat. We were picked on because we had to push a shopping cart full of clothes through the neighborhood in order to do laundry. We were both embarrassed and happy. Embarrassed because the neighborhood kids laughed at us as we pushed that heavy cart full of clothes. Happy because we would have clean clothes after months of dirty laundry. At other times we could not afford to go to the laundromat. My grandmother would say, "Gal, go get that pail and wash dem clothes." We dreaded that moment because that meant we had to be outside in the hot sun, washing clothes in this huge metal bucket with a washing board. Then, if that wasn't enough, we had to hang them on a clothesline to dry, but again, we had clean clothes, so those were happy days.

To think what you wore to school or had on would create so much misery was an understatement. Kids can be cruel. We were picked on for not having the best clothes, wearing the same shoes, and being smelly because a bath every night was not the norm for us either. We had days we were told to bathe because my grandma said you were not going to run her water bill up. It sounds so funny saying that now, but Pearl was serious about that water bill and any other bill for that matter; who could blame her, though? You are a woman trying to maintain a small home of at least seventeen people at any given time.

Kindergarten was also when my first fight (besides fighting my siblings and cousins) occurred. Although I was unkept, I was extremely smart for some reason. I always gave God credit for my photographic memory. It was the ability to recall everything that I read or saw that allowed me to excel in school. School was easy for me. The work came easy for me as well. Most times, I made straight A's but I never made anything less than the B honor roll. School was my place of refuge. Yep! This is why that fight occurred. I was accused of being the teacher's pet. Life is so funny, though. The same girl I had the fight with is still my friend. I call her "my day 1."

I also loved school lunch and breakfast. That may sound weird to some but I never missed breakfast or lunch because that was the time I could eat things besides what grandma cooked or gave us. So, it was in kindergarten that I discovered that what I saw as everyday life was not okay.

Kindergarten was also around the time that I realized it was not just my aunts and uncles that were on drugs, but my mother had also succumbed to that demon called crack as well. My mom was a little different, though. She was what you would call a functioning addict. She would still work and do whatever it took to take care of her kids. For that reason, every so often, she would find a place for us to live. She would say, "At least you have your own now." The problem with "having our own now" also meant most times, we went without lights, water, and the basic supplies for everyday living. I can remember going months at a time with no electricity or running water. What I realize now is she would never move too far from my grandma. Twice, we lived on the same street and one time a street over. The furthest we ever moved was about two miles away from Grandma's house to what we called crosstown. In other words, although she wanted her independence, she never went too far from home. Unfortunately, these bouts of her wanting to be independent and be on her own while still being addicted to crack is how the monsters gained access to us.

CHAPTER 3

MY TRUTH

I am by no means a doctor of psychology nor any other doctor for that matter. But we can all admit personal experience does not require a degree. No one can tell you more about a trauma they experienced than a Survivor. Yes, I choose the word SURVIVOR because I absolutely refuse to become anyone's victim. I am the first to admit though, that I was a victim for a very long time. However, one day after attending a sex trafficking event I heard the speaker refer to herself as a survivor. I decided that day to never again refer to myself as a victim, but a survivor.

When it comes to trauma, some have said, "I want to forget everything that happened." Especially the traumas caused by our childhood. As a Pastor, I have encountered people who have so deeply suppressed their childhood trauma that they really did not consciously remember what happened. It was not until we got to the root cause of their issues that they realized the majority of what they were experiencing Spiritually stemmed from a traumatizing event that they had subconsciously suppressed. I can truly say this has never been the case for me. I remember every incident like it was yesterday. I definitely go into each event with the full knowledge that it might just ruffle some feathers, but I have recently come to the knowledge of my own truths. One of my truths that I now acknowledge is the fact that I wanted to always ensure everyone is okay and their feelings are spared even at my own expense. It is one of the reasons it has taken me almost seven years to tell my story. Now I go in with the full understanding of knowing that telling my story is a continuation of my healing process. I know this part may sound strange to some when I say it. Many will think my healing process would be my number one priority for telling my truth, but it's not. What persuades me more than anything is the unction that I have received from God compelling me to complete this book. That assures me that someone needs to hear my story to bring clarity, understanding and healing to their own situation.

So, as I previously stated, access was gained by way of my mother's addiction. My mother was absolutely the best mother she knew how to be. In the words of my aunt, addicts are most times good people with bad habits. I personally will never understand how anyone could hate a parent. I guess I am that way because of the knowledge that God has given me to understand that none of us are perfect, we all make mistakes, and as parents, we do the absolute best we can when it comes to raising our kids. Granted, I understand all of our stories differ, and someone may feel I have every right not to like or love my mother or father. I challenge you, no matter what they did, how much it may hurt, and how hard forgiveness may seem, forgive anyway. Forgiveness is not about them. It really is about you. We will talk about that more during my healing process.

My first encounter was at the age of five. I can remember how he looked, how he dressed, and how he smelled. He was one of my mom's boyfriends at the time. Again, this was one of those occasions she decided to live independently of my grandmother's house. He begins his grooming process by showing me more attention than my sisters. Attention at that time was a big deal to me. I was the middle child and never really got that much attention due to there being so many of us around. So that personal attention to me was a big deal. It's as if this pervert had the pick of the litter as my mom had three girls. Sidenote: If you are a parent and you do not understand the term grooming and what it looks like I solicit you to learn. So, his grooming process not only included showing me more attention than the other kids but he would buy me things like candy, treats, and toys. That was followed by always having to pick me up or by telling me to come and sit on his lap. Once he got me comfortable, the pick-ups turned into sexual touching in my private areas. No matter who was in the room, he always

found ways to touch me. The biggest act
that made the most impression and caused
major trauma was the day he called us all
inside the room under the pretense of
playing a video game. It was the eighties,
and the Atari had just come out. The only
video games that we were used to at that
time, were the ones at Ms. Liz's game room
or the laundromat. Having a game right in
your home that you could plug right up to
the television was a big deal. That day, he
made sure I sat behind him. We were so
innocently excited because he bought us a
new game to play on the Atari. It was in
the midst of the game that he pulled me
closer to his back, pulled my panties to the
side, and began inserting his fingers inside
me. I had never felt anything like that

before. All I can remember is that it hurt, and I wanted him to stop. It sounds so crazy now as an adult writing this. I had to say to myself, as I am sure many others will say reading it, why didn't I just move, why did I not run and tell my mom? But, of course, these are things I can't answer and I will probably never know. I was five years old. These monsters have a way of making a child think they will be the ones to get in trouble or that they will hurt their parents by telling them what happened. It would be years later before I would see him again. The ironic part is how that encounter would become a major part of my healing process.

CHAPTER 4

From My Safe Place to My Hell

The smile on my face when my mom first introduced me to the man, she said would be my god-dad was priceless. I never really knew how they met. If he was simply a friend of the family or if he was someone she was dating. I still never understood why he was only my god-dad when I had two other sisters, but oh well. Life was funny that way in our family. When you are a child growing up less fortunate, not living in the best conditions, and not having the variety of foods you want, seeing this at someone else's home is a big deal. Now that I know better, I realize the way my god-dad lived was really pretty normal. But to a child growing up the way I did seeing his home clean and nice and the fridge full to capacity with different snacks and juices was new to me. I remember how excited I would get every time my mom told me I was about to spend the weekend with him. I can vaguely remember him having a girlfriend at one point. She would oftentimes be there as well. Many times, I went over to spend weekends without any incidents. My god-dad's home was my safe place. It was my time to be alone. I could watch my favorite cartoons and sitcoms. I was a child who loved television. I would get lost in cartoons like Heathcliff, Thunder Cats and The Smurfs.

My favorite sitcoms back then were *What's Happening, Happy Days, Good Times,* and *Night Rider*. Just to name a few. But I could get caught up in watching television at my god-dad's house without the worry of having to share that one television in grandma's living room. I laugh now and tell my children they just don't know how good they have it. A television in every room was something I could only dream of as a child. Furthermore, just having a room back then was a big deal. Anyhow, that black and white twelve-inch screen television my grandma had would not break for anything. It even fell one time, got cracked on the side and still worked. Grandma had an iron hanger in it to keep reception. Whenever the television would mess up and the hanger did not work, she would hit it to make the picture come back in. To this day, I will never understand how that worked. Either way, you were going to watch what was on. What she liked. Cereal or oatmeal and cartoons on Saturday morning, though, was one thing she made sure the kids were able to do.

Back to god-dad's house. So, because I was the only child there, it was all about me, that big color television and all the food I wanted. I never felt unsafe, and I truly loved my god-dad. I never really thought of him then as anything less than my actual dad. All of his kids by that time were older. I loved the thought of having older siblings. They spoiled me as well. They called me their little sister. They came over from time to time but did not live there. Nothing about my god-dad's house showed any signs of trouble or that there would be issues. I can't remember an exact time but I can surely say it was more than a year that visitations with my god-dad would take place. Then, the dreaded day came when my safe haven turned into my own private hell.

That afternoon, my god-dad and I left to go to the store. This day he told me I could only get one candy. I was used to just getting what I wanted but he was adamant that day about me only having one piece of candy. I still do not know what made me do this, but I decided I would take a small red

Jolly Rancher, put that in my mouth, and give my god-dad the green stick Jolly Rancher to pay for. Once he paid for it, I put that one in my mouth, too. By the time we got home, my god-dad said open your mouth. Immediately, I knew I was caught. Yep, it was my first time stealing, and I got caught. He said, "I bought you a green candy. Why is your mouth red and green." I knew I was in trouble. I got a real spanking that day. It is safe to say I never stole again.

After getting a spanking, my god-dad called me in his room to talk to me. He explained that he did not want to spank me, how stealing was not good, and that stealing could land me in jail. It was after this talk that he walked to the closet and started taking his clothes off. This is where it gets a little tricky. As a child, I still did not understand if this was an act and a part of the manipulation or if he actually made a mistake and did not know I was there. As he took off his pants, I screamed "Dad! I am still in here!" Immediately, he pulled his pants back up and apologized. He claims he did not know I was still in the room. But if he were truly sorry it would have ended there, but it didn't. It was at that moment that he once again fully exposed himself as he sat on the side of his bed with me. He began to explain the body parts of men and how they differ from that of women. He then asked me to touch it and play with it. As a child, I remember being so confused as to why the man I loved and saw as my dad would do something that made me so uncomfortable. Something I never wanted to do. He took pleasure in a child touching on him. He enjoyed it, while I simply wanted to disappear from the entire room. Of course, after that the instructions of not telling anyone came. He actually used the act of stealing against me. He threatened that if I told my mom or anyone what happened between us, he would tell her that I stole that piece of candy. So, of course, I kept that secret until my adulthood. Not because I was still afraid as an adult but I truly felt what's the point in bringing it up now. That was the unhealed version of me speaking. There are some parts of my god-dad and my safe place coming to an end that I obviously did suppress as I have no clue when I stopped visiting him as a child. I simply remember that I just never went again. Maybe it was my mom feeling something, or maybe it was his brother being accused of molesting another child not long after. Whatever it was I just realized there was nowhere that was safe for me and no man that could be trusted.

Notes/Reflection

CHAPTER 5

INNOCENSE LOST

I was ten years old when I first experienced sex. At this tender age, is when I experienced full-blown sex, penetration, rape, and incest. So far, you have heard my experience of molestation by being fondled and touched in private areas. Webster's Dictionary defines incest as sexual intercourse between persons so closely related that they are forbidden by law to marry. I describe incest as being violated by anyone who you respected or has always been known as part of the family to you.

This portion of my testimony is not about describing, naming, or even throwing hints about my offender. I chose to forgive them. So, this portion of my story is not about them. It is about me and my healing process. There is a serious taboo in the Black community regarding sexual predators. It is really sad to say, but all too often, we tend to do to the victim what we should be doing to the predator. We violate the victim all over again by saying some of the nastiest things. I have heard from victims who have been called liars, accused of being "too grown and fast," what took place is their fault, or they are simply not believed by those they felt should not only believe them but protect them. This needs to change in our community. I will continue to be a voice that helps with that change through my program "When Women Heal." So, my choice not to call the offender out is not about protecting them or my family dynamics. I choose not to because I have truly forgiven all my offenders. Mathew 6:14-15 tells us "If we can't forgive those that trespass against us, our heavenly Father will not forgive us our trespasses." This scripture is not up for debate for me. If the scripture would have ended with 'unless' then I could justify not forgiving them but it did not. Also, Luke 6:32-36 tells us how easy it is to love those who love us and do good to us but can we do the same towards our enemies? We can't just live the parts of the Bible we like and leave the other parts out. I always say,

"No one will send me to hell on a scholarship." In other words, I will not lose my crown and mansion God promises me for anyone. Therefore, I choose to follow the words of Christ and forgive my violators. This is the mentality that has caused me to not only be free but defeat the devil in this area of my life. This mindset positioned me to not allow trauma to dictate my life. I choose to use my experience to help others. What the devil meant for my harm turned out for my good (Romans 8:28).

I remember this just as plain as all my other experiences. My mother's addiction had once again disrupted my life. I had to go to live with other family members. It was not family I knew growing up so I had to be introduced to everyone. This family was different. They were middle class and had more material things than I was used to seeing. We did more, went places and always dressed for the occasion. I was so happy for the chance to experience and learn that there was way more to life than what I had been exposed to. Once again, I felt safe in my new environment. I felt as though I could breathe again and be a child. No more struggling. No more being an adult and having to change diapers and fix bottles for my younger cousins. No more struggling! It felt so good, but unfortunately, the overwhelming feeling of happiness would not last.

I had been in my new environment for over a year before anything ever occurred. I can't say it enough. I felt safe until, one day, I was left home alone with the person who would become my third offender. I did not realize this until I was an adult and got involved with sex trafficking that although the violation took time to occur, the grooming process began months in advance. For the sake of knowledge, I am compelled to stop here and explain what the "grooming process is." I have run into too many people who do not know or understand it. This is a term that every adult should know. Especially those with kids. I always say it's so dangerous being a parent, and you have never heard, or have no knowledge of grooming. This is one of the biggest reasons we have so many missing black and brown children. I will forever thank Jumorrow Terra Poitier and SheMeHer, Inc. for teaching this to not just me but to our community as a whole. It provoked me to become active.

According to Mrs. Poitier, who is the founder of SheMeHer, Inc., an organization that advocates for victims of sex trafficking, grooming is a deliberate process by which the offender gradually initiates and maintains a sexual relationship with victims in secrecy. Grooming is the process a predator uses to identify, manipulate, and ultimately control someone for the sole purpose of exploitation and/or sexual abuse.

Grooming allows offenders to slowly overcome boundaries long before sexual abuse occurs. Usually, the offender is well known and trusted by the child and parent or legal guardian. The perpetrator will start by targeting the child. It's usually a child who is vulnerable, has a need to be fulfilled, has a lack of parental oversight, or lives in a chaotic home. Next, they gain the child's trust as well as the trust of the child's guardian. Then, they will do things to fulfill the needs of the child. This may be done by buying things the child needs or doesn't get from their caregiver or by filling the void a child has, like missing their biological father. They will begin to see the person as someone who is there and cares. This act is not predicated on gender.

Violators can be male or female.   Once
trust is established, they begin to isolate the
child.   They can do this by volunteering to
babysit, taking the child to places they like
or think are fun, coaching them in sports,
and sadly, even asking them to volunteer to
assist at church.   Once the child becomes
dependent and feels they are loved by the
offender, that's when the sexual violations
begin.   Once the violation occurs the
offender will now begin to threaten the
child in an attempt at controlling the
narrative. This is usually done by making
threats to the child or blaming them for
what happened. This causes the child to be
afraid to tell their caregiver. I can attest to
this as my mother did not find out about my
violation until I was an adult. There are so

many components surrounding molestation and incest. Please do your part (especially parents) in learning more about the grooming process. I am not a professional. I am simply sharing the things I have learned but, more importantly, what I have experienced.

Now back to where we left off. After the grooming process was complete and I was left home alone with my offender for the first time, is when it all started. I was taken into the room. Fear immediately came over me as I was all too familiar with that look. The look of knowing what he was about to do. The look of knowing it's wrong but not having the power to resist that sexual demon inside. He began by touching my private area. That happened to me before, and although uncomfortable it was grossly familiar. Nothing, however, could have prepared a ten-year-old for what was about to happen next. The offender placed me in a position on my hands and knees, and my clothes were pulled down. I could not see as my offender was behind me, nor did I understand what was happening. The next thing I knew, I felt an immense pain like nothing I had ever experienced. That's when I realized this was another level of sex. This was full-blown penetration. I tried to move, but he kept pulling me back. He seemed to get pleasure out of forcing his too-large penis into a child. All I could think was, how can a person that is supposed to be family do such a thing?

Thank God I had not started menstruation at that time because I could have easily been impregnated as a child. I remember crying for a full week. I remember feeling so nasty and unworthy. The spirit of depression immediately overtook me. I was angry once again at my mother as I blamed her and her addiction for being there.

The violations continued for a while. No one around me even took notice of how I would react when I was left alone with him. No one paid attention. I will never forget wanting it to come to an end. So, I finally built up the courage and nerve to tell my caregiver. I might as well have kept it to myself because absolutely nothing was done besides them saying, "You better not be messing with that girl." Of course, he lied and said he was not. The feeling of no concern, no accountability, and not being believed felt almost as bad as the violation itself. Like many families in our community life just simply went on.

I am happy to say my mother got saved, cleaned up her act, and stopped using drugs. That was the last time I was violated. It was not the last time someone attempted to groom me, but the last time I was violated. I was twelve years old and there were several attempts after that with the grooming process, but by then, I was a force to be reckoned with. I was forced to grow up fast. I was strong-minded and strong-willed. I absolutely refused to be violated EVER again!

CHAPTER 6

DAMAGED GOOD

I had made up my mind that I would never be violated again. The part I was not prepared for, nor did I understand, was the mental damage that was done as a result of molestation and incest. Many victims battle demons within themselves. Some understand, receive therapy, and choose to heal from the trauma. Unfortunately, many don't even understand where they are mentally, physically, or spiritually after being violated. Again, I am not a professional. Everything I say is from my personal experience. With that being said,

I have witnessed that molestation and incest create three different people a victim can become. There are many more attributes besides these three, but as an advocate in the community as well as a pastor, these are the three I have dealt with the most. The three people created by incest and molestation are the angry person, the "trust no one" person, and the promiscuous person. The angry person is usually full of rage. They see everything through broken lenses. They are not okay and usually lash out at any and everybody for the least thing. They do not know any other way to free themselves of their own thoughts, so they act out through anger. I pay close attention to angry people. Especially little girls. It is so important that we ask questions as parents and not just assume the child is just "bad." There is a possibility that it could be so much more like molestation. Then you have the "trust no one" person. These victims usually have a lack of trust for most people around them. They feel that no one can be trusted and everyone is out to get them. They have the need to control every aspect of their life and environment. Control becomes a big part of their makeup. They are extremely anti-social. Then there is the promiscuous person. I can go much further in-depth with this attribute because I became that person. Although I dealt with anger and trust issues, promiscuity was the biggest demon I battled.

Unfortunately, I became a promiscuous person as a result of being victimized. Most of the people who know me and read this will find it hard to believe, but, yes, its who I was as a result of molestation. This is my truth. I often tell people, "Do not judge a person by what you see. Especially when you do not know their WHY." I never knew the cause of why I was so sexually active until my healing process. I did not have anyone to say to me, "Hey, this is not you. There is a deeper-rooted issue that needs to be resolved." No one ever said 'Why do you have a different man every time we turn around?" Instead, they just laughed and talked behind my back. Even the ones who called themselves saints of God would speak curse words over my life and say how many babies I would have. Glad to say they lied because I only had one biological son. Was what they were saying about me true? Absolutely, but I wonder if the narrative would have changed if they knew my WHY! What if they had simply asked and realized I was damaged goods from being violated as a child?

I became voluntarily sexually active at the age of fifteen. My boyfriend then thought he was taking my innocence. He thought I was a virgin because that's what I told him. Little did he know my innocence had been lost since the age of five. Being sexually active became natural to me. I remember an older woman once told me, "Once the faucet has been turned on it's pretty hard to turn it off." Well, my faucet had been turned on, and I cared even less about it being turned off. Sex felt good to me. It made me feel loved and wanted. I got pleasure out of satisfying men sexually. I did not care about them or their feelings. I did not have the attributes of a nurturing, caring woman. To be brutally honest I was worse than a man that played women. I would even brag about wanting nothing from a man but sex and money. This is when I learned that it was not about looks as I was more overweight than I am now. But it was about confidence. That's how I attracted some pretty good-looking men. I was even more intrigued with men who had the same mentality as me. Let's be friends and have sex. No commitment was my thing. I actually ran from commitment. The funniest thing was I hated men deep down inside, but my desire for sex made me love their company. It was extremely hard to fuel my sex drive. That was one of the reasons I had multiple partners. I would never let any of them get too close. I think there may have been one or two men that I really cared about then, but no relationship ever lasted. I didn't want them to. I was going through life masking my pain, sabotaging relationships, and acting out through sex. Parents, again it is so important that you ask questions if you have a child acting out sexually.

I was nineteen when I got involved with a married man. It was my way of being able to get sex when I wanted it and not having to worry about the aggravation of questions and quality time. I know it sounds crazy, as quality time is what most women desire. I love quality time now, but I certainly did not then. Just remembering the level of disrespect towards this man's wife saddens me today. But back then, I was young, angry, and damaged. I did not care. It never crossed my mind for a second the chaos I was causing in someone else's life. This was normal to me as I was conceived by a married man, and so were my two siblings. It was nothing in my family for a woman to date a married man. We were never taught how wrong it was, so I never even questioned it. But one thing you can always count on is you will definitely reap what you sow, and boy did I reap. I also found out how important it is to break generational curses. We will discuss that later though. I was consumed with the fact that I had someone in my life who gave me what I wanted with no form of commitment. Sex and happiness were the name of the game and he fulfilled my desires. It was eight years before that relationship ended. Of course, it ended because he became way too clingy. A man is not what I was looking for. It was the satisfaction of my flesh alone. There was something about possession and ownership of me and my body by a man that was totally off-limits. I did not know it then, but I understand now it was the effects of molestation and incest. I was damaged mentally, and no one recognized it.

CHAPTER 7

THE FIRST INVITE

So, I am sure by now you are wondering who and what was invited in. Molestation and incest open up a flood of feelings and emotions that sometimes can't even be explained. There are times that you will feel on top of the world, like you have everything in your life under control. Then, there are other times when you become emotional, depressed, and sad. You feel like your entire life is falling apart. I am sure there are many victims who understand this all too well, and others may have felt this and much more. I myself never became suicidal, but I know victims who are really close to me who actually attempted suicide. No victim nor their feelings are ever the same again, this is why they should never be judged or persecuted.

The first invite started with my first marriage. I met my first husband at the end of 2001. By May of 2002, we were married. I did not realize it then, but the effects of abuse would join me in this marriage. Have you ever heard the saying "Broken people attract broken people?" That's what happened with my first marriage and future relationships. The marriage was completely broken before it ever even started. First of all, we eloped. It was three months before my parents and siblings found out I was married. My husband convinced me to keep it a secret. I was in love, and he had an ulterior motive; he simply needed a green card. I went from being the player to getting played. For the first time, I let my guard down. I loved this man, and he completely took advantage of that love. There were many signs, but like most broken people, I chose to ignore them. Another problem was I believed in God, and he didn't. I tried to help him understand who God was and why we should believe. He would make jokes and say he did not care if he went to hell; he would just party down there with the rest of his homeboys. My body would cringe every time he said it. Eventually, I just stopped talking about God with him altogether, not for my sake, but his. He would make comments about God I dare not repeat. Once again, I did not understand then what I understand now. I had a soul tie before I ever got married. I loved him, and I just wanted to fix it.

That's where the manifestation of the effects of molestation first began in my marriage. I invited the "I can fix it" spirit in. No matter what he did, I just knew if I tried hard enough, I could "fix it." It was funny to me how I went from not caring about a man or his feelings to the next stage of falling so deep for a man that I was willing to accept any and everything from him. I went from being numb and not giving affection to wanting and craving it from someone else. It was all so confusing to me. I was twenty-four years old in a toxic relationship. This is where that reaping from dating a married man came in. Some like to believe that life just simply happens. No, life does not just happen. There are many elements involved, and reaping and sowing is one. Most like to call it karma, but the Bible calls it reaping and this man was definitely the tool used to make it happen.

Our relationship started out as a lie. I was out clubbing when I met him. He was with a group of guys, and I was with a group of ladies. I remember having so much fun outside with them that we never even made it inside the club. The next day, I called him and we spoke for hours on the phone. We did this for the entire week. By Friday, he asked if I would come see him. When I got to his house and he came out I realized he was not the person who had given me his phone number. I mean, he was the guy that I had been talking to on the phone, but he was definitely not the guy I remember meeting. I said to him you are not the guy I met that night. He swore to me he was. It was not until his brother got off work and came home that I screamed, "You lied! He is the one who I met that night." They both laughed and thought it was so funny. He claimed he was too shy to approach me, so he sent his brother over instead. I should have seen the signs of dishonesty then.

Unfortunately, I was young and naïve and paid it no mind.

We began to date and see each other very often. He lived with his brother, his girlfriend, and their two kids. One day while visiting, a conversation emerged about bills and how hard it was to maintain the apartment they lived in. Again, looking for a way to help "fix it," I volunteered to move in with them. I figured my income, along with theirs, would keep him from having so much financial difficulty. I remember telling my parents. Lord, they were old-school Christians. Telling them I was moving in with my boyfriend did not go over well at all. They warned me I needed to be careful. They told me I did not know him well enough to be moving in with him and I needed to slow down. They told me I should not go and "shack up" with a man. That's what the old folks called living with a person you are in a relationship with, but not married to. As with most young adults, I did not want to hear anything they had to say. My mind was made up. I moved in a few days later. I was so excited to be out of my parent's house in my own space. It was not the first time I had lived on my own, but it was my first time living with a man. I enjoyed doing all the things for him that I had been taught to do. The problem was I was taught to do it for a husband and not a boyfriend. Anyhow, everything was going so well. We worked during the week and partied on the weekends. I was having the time of my life with him.

One night while lying in bed, he turned and said, "I want us to get married." To be honest I laughed because I thought he was joking. He said, "No I am serious I need to get married." I gave him this strange look. I did not understand what he meant by he needed to. Most people who get married want to. He began to tell me in an emotional voice that he was in the U.S. on a work visa. If he did not get married, he would have to leave and go back to Guatemala. The news hit me like a ton of bricks. The idea of losing the love of my life, the one I was having so much fun with, the one I thought cared for me so much did not sit well with me. So, here I go again," It's ok honey, we can "fix that." I told him I could not stand the thought of losing him and I would marry him. The smile he gave me melted my heart. It assured me I was doing what was best for both of us. I am almost embarrassed to say this, but, a month later, we caught the city bus to the courthouse and got married. No family, wedding, reception, not even a vacation. We just caught that city bus and eloped. I was foolishly in love.

It was not long after we got married that the trouble in paradise began. I first noticed how he would take phone calls outside and stay on the phone for a long time. When I asked who he was talking to there was always an excuse, "Oh it's my mom." "Oh, my son wanted to talk." Although every fiber in my being knew he was lying, I would not question it. It went from hours on the phone to late nights out. At first, I ignored it. I acccpted the excuse of just hanging out with the boys. Lord knows there is something about a woman and our natural intuition. We can pick up in our spirit when something is wrong in a relationship. Even when we do not confront it right away and even refuse to believe it—we know. At first, I refused to believe it. I refused to rock the boat by making accusations against him. Once again, I made myself believe that I could "fix it." I told myself if I gave him all my attention, had more exotic sex, and partied with him more that things would get better. None of it worked. It got worse. The late nights turned into not coming home at all. I cried and beat myself up, wondering how I could be so stupid to let my guard down. I was angry with myself for allowing him in. I told myself if I had stayed a player, I would never have been in this position. It was then that I made up my mind that two could play this game.

I had been raised in the church. I knew what the sanctity of marriage was and how important it was to God. I knew that adultery was a sin. I did not care. I was hurting, and I wanted him to feel just as much pain and hurt as I was feeling. I begin to kindle old relationships. I would never sleep away from home like he would, but I did what I wanted and when I wanted to. Although I knew by now that he was seeing other women, he never did anything in my face. One night we were at his friend's birthday party. I started seeing people whisper and give me looks. That was the other thing. My husband was Hispanic, so conversations could take place without me understanding what was being said. So, as people talked, I was clueless. It was not until the end of the night that I finally put two and two together. His mistress was at the party, and it did not take me long to figure it out. Well, back then I was a fighter, and it went all the way down. It took him and almost five of his friends to hold me back. Yes, five! Those who know,

know. You would think after all of this I would be done, but nope. Knowing and seeing are two different things. Knowing hurt me. To actually see her in some strange way motivated me. It became a competition of 'may the best woman win.' The fact that she was deathly afraid of me made it worse. It fueled me. I was seeking her out to fight her. In my head, this was winning. The game of 'may the best woman' win went on for two years. I thought because he never left home, I was winning. Never thinking he had a reason not to. His status in the country was more important than either of us.

The game I thought I was winning turned out to be the biggest loss. I found out his mistress was pregnant. That was a blow so hard to me that it took my breath away. The news came months after the doctors told me that, more than likely, the way my cervix was built, I would never be able to conceive. I was done with the game. But I vowed to go out with a bang. Again, I was still too young and naïve to realize I wasn't hurting him. I was only hurting myself. Either way, in my head, I was going to do my big one. Since nothing I seemed to do made a difference to him, I did something that I knew would hurt him. I started talking to his best friend. We all know homeboys are off-limits, but at this point, nothing was off-limits. No matter what I had to do, I was going to make him feel the pain I felt. I waited until he found out about us to move out.

Even after I moved out, we were still married, and we would still see each other. During our separation, I would be introduced to people, men, and women alike. I never thought anything about it. I would still spend nights with him and go out and have fun. I remember when my husband had to move, and living with me was certainly not an option. When I first went to his new place, I saw he was living with his cousin and her daughter. I would spend time at the house, and most weekends, I stayed overnight. Living separately but still married became our new norm. We were both okay with it. He dated whom he wanted, and I dated whom I wanted. The arrangement was weird to some, but it worked and kept the peace for us. One day I decided to go and see his brother's girlfriend. We had always been really close. She was even my confidential informant on a few occasions. But I could never prepare myself for the news she was about to reveal. We had been talking for a little while. Their kids were our God kids, so I spent some time with them. I was saying my goodbyes when she gave me this look. She said I have to tell you the truth. I cannot call myself a friend and know this information. She did not know until recently that my husband and I were still together but not living together. This was a bombshell. She explained that the woman my husband was living with, the woman I had thought was his cousin all these years, was actually his girlfriend. This man had me sleeping with him and spending the night at his girlfriend's house. I was so lost and confused. As having a baby in our marriage was not enough, he now had me in a whole sister-wives relationship! That was it! I was mad and ready to fight. I drove aimlessly around the city, going from house to house looking for both of them. By this time, one of their friends let them know I was aware of what was going on and I was on the prowl for both of them. They were afraid to go home. I waited for hours trying to locate them. I know right now, until this very day, that God did not allow me to find them. I am totally transparent when I say I know without a shadow of a doubt I would have caught a case. That was my mindset on that day. I saw red! This all took place on a Saturday. By Monday, my husband began blowing my phone up. I refused to answer. Finally, I got tired and answered. I was so emotional. All I remember was cursing him out. He began to beg and plead for me to just listen to him. I yelled and said, "I have nothing to talk to you about!" and hung up on him. If I had known those would be my final words to him forever, it may have been different. My final words to my husband were, "I have nothing to say to you." Every emotion I carried, all the anger and resentment from wounds that never healed bled out on him in one day.

September 1, 2005, at 3:10 pm, six days after finding out about Juan's infidelity and four days after hanging up in his face, I was leaving work and had not made it a block when I received a phone call. It was Missy. Her voice cracked as she said, "Shantel, they need you to go to the medical examiner's office. Juan fell from a building at work. He is dead." I wish she had taken the time to ask me if I was sitting or who was around me because, at that moment, I almost crashed my car. I had to pull into a parking lot to gather myself. I bawled for an hour in that parking lot. It would be years before I forgave myself. I vowed never to walk in unforgiveness again no matter what. After Juan's death, I found out so many more things. His funeral was like a freefall. His mistress showed up along with her coworkers and friends. It was sad as well as hilarious how many of her coworkers thought it was her husband who passed. Of course, being as vocal as I was back then, I made it known that she was the mistress and not his wife. I never knew how things were for her when she went back to work at that hospital, but I could only imagine. I also found out that day that she was not the only woman who I thought was a cousin of Juan's, but were his girlfriends as well. One of them had even lived in our home. It's funny how people will wait until someone has passed before telling everything they know about that person's lifestyle. Especially the things that were done wrong. So much more came out that my attorney, at the time, asked if he could write a book. I did not realize then the book, the story of my life, was nowhere near complete.

CHAPTER 8

THE INVINCIBLE WALL

You would think after all I subjected myself to with my 'fix it mentality' I would seek some sort of professional or spiritual help, but I didn't. I kept going about my life, still getting involved in toxic relationships, still trying to fix broken people, and still experiencing life with broken lenses. One of those broken relationships was with my son's father. We never got married or engaged. We were simply friends with benefits because I built a wall so tall over my heart that serious relationships became a big no again. He was a great friend to me. We were able to talk about anything. He knew where I stood and I knew where he stood. He was just as broken as I was as a result of past relationships. It was great to me, though at that time. We understood that commitment was not an option for either of us. We went out on dates, talked on the phone about our problems for hours, and, of course, we slept together. That is what really tied us together. Things were going well with this arrangement. I was able to have a man in my life but still protect myself from the hurt and pain that was caused by my past.

Remember when the doctor said that I could not have a baby, well apparently, they were wrong because a baby was on the way. The ironic part is, we had just watched the movie "Knocked Up." We laughed so hard during the movie not knowing I was literally knocked up. I've never been able to understand how instantly my feelings changed. I went from being okay with our friends with benefits relationship to falling in love at the news of having this man's child. Of course, none of it ended well. Although we tried making it work and having a good parental relationship, we just could not get past how our relationship started. Now instead of a wall around my heart, there was a full fortress. It is important that I emphasize how happy I am to have my miracle baby. He is now a teenager and we have the best bond ever. He truly taught me what love without limits looks like.

By the time that chapter of my life was over, I was ready to fully surrender to God. So, in 2010, when my son was only one, I did just that. I became so serious about God no one stood a chance. I was on my way to healing spiritually and it felt great. My child and my relationship with Christ became my top priority. God placed pastors in my life who were able to identify my pain. I forgave myself for what happened between Juan and I, and came to grips with that dreadful day of not listening to him and hanging up instead. I was able to come to grips with not knowing what he wanted to say to me before he died. My mind was healed from replaying it in my head over and over. I was a single mother, an entrepreneur, and fulfilling my ministry works. Life was looking up, and my future was looking so much brighter.

For almost three years I remained focused. I no longer felt the need to be validated by a man. Every soul tie had been broken, and I was good being saved, single, and celibate. There is something about abstaining from sex as you strengthen your relationship with God. You no longer allow your feelings and emotions to lead, instead you take full control of them. I was healing and being made whole. God had corrected my lenses, and I saw so much clearer. I was able to see how my promiscuous lifestyle was the result of molestation and incest. I am a firm believer that in order to heal from anything, it is important to know the root cause of the issue.

During this time, I was so passionate about others being saved; I wanted them to be just as happy as I was. I invited everyone to church who would come. One day an ex, Bernie, contacted me and said he was going through a really hard time. He learned that I was saved and had gotten my life together. He asked if I could pick him up for church. Allow me to be transparent, although I'm happy to hear about anyone wanting to go to church, I felt no desire to take him. I told him there were a thousand churches in his area and he should pick one of them. Sometimes I wish I had stuck to that response, but I realize now that some things in life are a necessary part of your journey. That does not mean I jumped and said yes, either. I told him I would pray about it and let him know. I completely disliked the idea of letting any man from my past into my new space. I was enjoying my relationship with God, and that was all I needed. I did not realize it until he called again, but it had been two weeks since I told him I would pray about picking him up for church. This time he begged and said to me it was a matter of life and death. After telling my leaders what had occurred and what he said, they advised me to pick him up and bring him. Their words to me were, "God forbid something happens; you do not want his blood required to your hands." Meaning, that if I did not bring him to church and he lost his life, I could be the blame because God was using me to help him. So, I listened to their counsel and invited him to church.

Bernie was doing well at church. He gave his life to Christ, and attended every service we had. Equally important, my son was having so much fun with him. He would bring a treat every time we went to church, which at that time was three times a week. This may sound funny, but the other reason he and my son were getting close is I refused to let him sit in the front seat with me. I was so saved. I took everything my leaders said literally. Our pastor once preached that single people don't need to ride to church together because someone may accidentally touch a leg and set things off. No one was setting anything off around me so in that back seat he went without care or hesitation. I still laugh just thinking about how religious I was.

Bernie became very helpful. He was doing so well at church that I started feeling comfortable enough to let him come over and do things around the house instead of paying someone to do it. I would even cook him meals as he worked around the house. I was still focused, but at the same time, I was happy to have a man help around the house and help with my son. He would make any excuse to come over. There was always something around the house that needed fixing. One day, he says, "I am going to marry you." Further, he said, "Not right now because I am getting myself together, but one day soon, we are going to get married." I brushed it off and said, "Yea right."

A few days later, I picked Bernie up for church as I had done three times a week for a little over a month. It was on our usual Bible study night, and my habit was to clean the church after service. I was sweeping the floor as Bernie talked to our Bishop. Then I notice Bishop with this huge smile on his face. It was at that moment that Bernie walked over, dropped on one knee, with no ring, and asked me to marry him. I was speechless and angry all at the same time. No, I was not happy. Yes, I wanted to say no. I could not understand why he asked me to marry him, and we had not so much as gone on a date, that is, unless he considered these days at church a date. Otherwise, I was lost. By this time, everyone had been told I was being proposed to and they all came running back into the church. Not only was I shocked, but being watched by about twenty-five people. I guess he saw the look in my eyes, and immediately said, "Bishop told me to ask you." It may sound strange, but at that time, I was so influenced by my leaders that hearing those words alone made me say 'yes.' Everyone clapped while I stood there in shock, so shocked that I had gone through an entire proposal with the broom and dustpan still in my hand. Everyone clapped and celebrated. My old church was very big on marriage, it was called the marrying church. It was a huge deal. That night we all sat around for at least an hour with everyone congratulating us. I was asked by one of my church sisters if I felt love. My answer was, "I guess." Something definitely shifted with my feelings that felt like love but really, I was unsure.

The following day I remember waking up excited about being engaged. Not because it was good for me but simply because my church family was so happy. I had heard so much about the importance of marriage that I felt marriage was the ultimate accomplishment. Again, marriage was a big deal in my church. Most couples even followed our leaders by dressing in the same colors. Being single or staying engaged was not celebrated like marriage was. Sundays were always a packed-out service for our church. Bernie and I were called to the front of the church, and the announcement was made that we were engaged; there was an even bigger celebration. Music was played, we danced, and received hugs from the congregation. This was even more reassuring that maybe it was the best thing for me. There was no dating period. We had a short counseling session over dinner that Sunday with our leaders, and by the next Tuesday night, we had a small marriage ceremony after Bible study. Yes, you got it right. We rode together to church for about a month, got engaged, and married in a week. The healing process can be funny. There are some wounds you will not know are still there until the scab gets peeled off. Little did I know that the fortress I had built around my heart, the invincible wall, was very much intact.

CHAPTER 9

THE FINAL INVITE

I remember waking up the day after our wedding night and looking over and seeing him lying beside me. There was really a man in my bed and I was not dreaming. This was real. I was a married woman. I remember feeling like my head was on a swivel. I was just single, saved, and happy last month. One month later, I am sitting here, married, and sharing my life and space with this man. It was a lot to process, and I had very little time to do it. I felt as though I had been on a wild roller coaster ride. But again, we were in love, and I was enjoying our new beginnings. He had a great job. I hit six figures for the first time in business and although I have never been a materialistic person, we were able to afford a nice home and vehicles. I was so confident that I had made the right decision when I listened to my leaders.

Bernie was an extremely affectionate man. He had no problem expressing that affection publicly. I never like using this word, so I never use it lightly. I absolutely hated the display of public affection, let alone more public displays like kissing or hugging. I had never been exposed to this, so I would have never known how much I had an issue with it until I encountered it. This is one of those scabs that I mentioned previously. My dislike for affection was too big of a deal not to notice. Bernie would become extremely angry about it. He could not understand why I did not want to be touched. I know you might be saying I thought you were once promiscuous and loved sex. Yes, I was, and I did. Being a victim of molestation and incest will not always be understood by those who have never experienced it. Victims can like and even love sex, but there are certain sexual acts that will trigger us. I never knew up to this point that the show of affection and touching without my consent was a trigger for me, but I would quickly find out.

One thing I realize about many people is they never want to admit their role in the demise of a relationship. I learned that admitting my role helped with healing. The more affection he tried to show, the more distant I became. I loved our sex life, but I hated the unwanted and unsolicited touching. I remember one day, I was standing at the sink washing dishes. The next thing I knew, I felt a touch on my backside. It was Bernie standing behind me at the kitchen sink. Now again, to most people that would be normal and appreciated by most wives, but not me. The fact that he had snuck up behind me and touched my butt set me completely off. I yelled at him to the top of my lungs. I asked him why he did that as if he was a strange man who walked into my home off the streets. I could see the hurt in his eyes.

He just looked at me and walked away. There was another time when I was asleep in bed. He was being playful and acting as though he was taking pictures of me while I was sleeping. Of course, I did not know or even cared to understand that it was just a joke. All I know is when I opened my eyes and saw him with that phone pointed at me, I totally lost it on him. I screamed, yelled, and even cried. I accused him of trying to get inappropriate pictures of me. Even after he showed me the phone wasn't unlocked, I still yelled and screamed. See, Bernie was aware that the presence of anyone standing near me or even walking in our room woke me up. So, to him, this was all fun and games; to me, it was a violation. There were so many more instances where I shunned his affection. People would see me push him away at church or family gatherings and ask me why I did him that way. There was no way I could explain it. It was not a conversation to have with anybody, and it surely wasn't a public conversation. His displays of affection and touching became so overwhelming to me that I sought the advice of my leader. One thing I will always give her credit for is God used her to pull me out of some really tough places, and healing from incest and molestation was one of them. Once again, the demons of my past had reared their ugly heads in my marriage. This time in the form of control and not wanting to be touched.

I thought I was healed. I thought molestation and incest would no longer have room in my life. Now, I was dealing with yet another level of this demon. I had once again invited a spirit into my marriage. I had taken the touch of my violators into my marital bed. It was then, almost two years into my marriage, that I realized the fortress previously built around my heart was still there. I stood at the altar and made vows before God but had never properly healed. My husband wanted all of me yet never even fully had a portion of me. He never got passed that wall around my heart.

When you love someone, and you are truly in love with them, you will fight for them.

You will change the things about yourself that you know can be detrimental to you and the other person. So, as soon as I noticed how my actions were affecting him, I dealt with it head-on. I did what was necessary to heal, which included counseling. One of the hardest things for me to deal with was control. Other victims I have spoken with have dealt with this as well. Having control can be good in some situations, but it has absolutely no space in marriage. The controlling spirit became comfortable to me. It was my way of protecting myself. Slowly I was able to let it go and trust God with all things. That is the reason why Proverbs 3:5-6 is one of my favorite verses, "Trust in the Lord with all your heart; and lean not unto your own understanding. In all thy ways acknowledge Him, and He will direct thy path." I have and will forever stand firmly on these verses. Things got better and can get better if we go slow. I want to stress that this was in no way a quick process I was able to open up to him. I started to be okay with the 'just because I love you touches.'

Although my marriage ended in divorce, which you can read about in my upcoming book, *Stay Out of God's Business: A Kingdom Love Story*. I could honestly say I came out healed from the spirits of molestation and incest. I had managed to break a generational curse that touched four generations. My healing was even tested one day after seeing one of my offenders at a traffic light. Remember I told you how one encounter would become a part of my healing process. Well, this was it! I had not seen that man in decades. The first thought I had was wanting to do harm to him. That is when I heard a still small voice ask, "Are you truly healed?" That is the day I forgave him and the two other offenders. I purposed in my heart that I would never again give anyone so much power that they could dictate my feelings, emotions, and the woman I had become. Forgiveness is not always easy, but it becomes easy once you realize the freedom that comes along with it. Forgiveness does not mean I have to have a one-on-one conversation with the person I am forgiving. It doesn't even mean that I ever have to see them again. It simply means that I properly position my heart through Christ, pardon their offense, and release them. I would urge any victim to release and forgive the offender. It is not for them; it is to free you. It is the beginning of your healing process. It's okay if you can't right now but pray about it until you can. Your true healing depends on it. BE YE HEALED!

Notes/Reflection

_____
_____
_____
_____
_____
_____
_____
_____
_____
_____
_____
_____
_____
_____
_____
_____
_____
_____
_____
_____
_____
_____
_____

Notes/Reflection

_____
_____
_____
_____
_____
_____
_____
_____
_____
_____
_____
_____
_____
_____
_____
_____
_____
_____
_____
_____
_____
_____
_____
_____
_____

Notes/Reflection

_____
_____
_____
_____
_____
_____
_____
_____
_____
_____
_____
_____
_____
_____
_____
_____
_____
_____
_____
_____
_____
_____
_____
_____
_____

Notes/Reflection

_____

_____

_____

_____

_____

_____

_____

_____

_____

_____

_____

_____

_____

_____

_____

_____

_____

_____

_____

_____

_____

_____

_____

_____

_____

Notes/Reflection

_____
_____
_____
_____
_____
_____
_____
_____
_____
_____
_____
_____
_____
_____
_____
_____
_____
_____
_____
_____
_____
_____
_____
_____

Made in the USA
Columbia, SC
18 November 2024

46013089R00067